D0885438

Wild Empty Spaces

Poems for the Opening Heart

"These are beautiful poems, written by a man who is uncompromising in his longing for freedom, truth, and beauty. They are a summons to go deeper, to play with wild abandon, to love with more passion, and to die to all conventions that keep us small and imprisoned." —Bruce Sanguin, Author of *The Way of the Wind: The Path and Practice of Evolving Christian Mysticism*

"In the tradition of Mary Oliver and David Whyte, Vince Gowmon has a powerful, compelling voice that speaks to the ecstasy and pain of living an awakened life. This book of poetry is a courageous, engaging, and daring invitation to dive deep into the body and belly of one's being, a wise, soul stirring yet playful companion to life's journey." —Eva DiCasmirro, Somatic Psychotherapist

"This collection of poetry is a rallying cry for the heart. With his bold and playful style, Vince Gowmon inspires us to dig deeper into truth and beauty and stretch beyond what we believe it means to be alive. These are poems you can return to again and again, discovering new treasures of meaning and insight each time." —Eric Bowers, Author of *Meet Me In Hard-to-Love Places: The Heart and Science of Relationship Success*

Also by Vince Gowmon

Let the Fire Burn ~ *Nurturing the Creative Spirit of Children*

Wild Empty Spaces

Poems for the Opening Heart

Vince Gowmon

2017
CREATIV PRESS
Vancouver, British Columbia, Canada
www.VinceGowmon.com

First published in 2017
by Creativ Press
Vancouver, BC, Canada

Contact information for Creativ Press can be found at
www.VinceGowmon.com.

ISBN: 978-0-9938595-4-0

Printed in the United States of America.

Text design, layout and cover design by Anna Wolff.

To my parents,

for their love,
their courage,
their fierceness,
their perfect imperfections,

all shaping the gifts
I was born to give.

The world will never give you what you want.

Only an open heart can.

CONTENTS

IV. Relating

~

~

V. Slowing

VI. Returning

Wild Empty Spaces

Poems for the Opening Heart

CAN YOU BE HERE IN THE EMPTINESS?

Can you be here in the emptiness?

Where the heart is open
and the mind is clear
the body wants nothing
and you're open to hear
a sound in the wind
a brush of a tree
the storm of the night
the voice beyond the dream.

Can you be here in the emptiness?

Where over the days
and over the years
it's been calling to you
beyond your fears
come back to this moment
come back right now
come back from your dream
it's here life is found.

Can you be here in the emptiness?

Where you stop searching
and finally let go
of all your ambitions
and all you think you know
of what you've sought after
and what you thought true
of everything you are
and everything you do.

There's nothing more
for you here now
there's nothing left to seek
all around.

Can you be here in the emptiness?

Leaving the dream
is all you've had to do
to let go of it all
and remember your truth:

You are nothing more
than endless love
an infinite speck
of timeless love
a drop of water
and a pool of light
a powerful presence
that shines so bright
a loving heart
an open mind
a beautiful gift
for all to find.

My gift to you
is for you to know
there's nothing to do
and nowhere to go
it's all in your heart
just let it come through
your truth, your joy
the love that is you.

Can you be here in the emptiness?

I. ARRIVING / BEGINNING

FALLING

I dreamt one night
that I was a leaf
lost in the wind,

yet I didn't realize
I was being carried
towards lands
needing me,

falling closer,
falling apart,
I died in their arms.

PROFOUND CRY

You are the child of a
shining world

a dream of a forgotten
dreamer

dreamt long ago

when you fell deep
into yearning

overwhelmed
to overflow

with inextinguishable unbounded
joy

an intense desire to share
to give

a profound cry
like that of a mother giving birth
screaming
to far away reaches
of everything you are
everything that is

an ancient wind rippling
exhaled
touching ground

alas
a dream set free

for others to feel
be moved by

if only for a
brief glimpse of time

an old faithful friend
reminding us
as all children do
of what's always been.

MINE TO CARRY

I turned to find
her
but she wasn't there

the faithful song
I came to depend on
no longer crooning me
through cold restless
nights

cradling arms
this nest I laid
so safely in
fallen from sight

I hung
by a thread
barely
dangling

right on the
fine edge of existence

where light touches
dark

a fleeting glimpse
in night's eye

pain
searing in my chest

the perennial sword
plundered

the deepest wound
is to the
human heart

the source
of all other wounds

this sword
its hilt
worn by age
bloodied with time

now handed to me
next on the line

this sacred inheritance

once hers

now mine to carry.

i-LAND

When the mind
separated from the body
man waged war
with himself.

will was born

Within the i
we find the secret,

the head disembodied,
floating above,

an island
lost at sea.

Worlds were built
on this i-land,
this little spec
of life,

worlds we thought
important

for thought built them
in the first place,

thought
lost in
thought
lost in
thought,

a prideful dream of sorts
with bridges and high-rises,
malls and schools,

where children were raised
upwards
into the little dot,

made to grow *up*
quickly,

manufactured into little thoughtful
workers
designed to feed those
feasting structures,

to become productive rational citizens
within this segregated colony
everyone seemed so
agreeable towards.

"Success" it was called.

This was life now.

Young ones fought
being shipped away
from their native land,

some quietly,
some vehemently,

disobedient,
disruptive,

struggling to focus
their soft attention,

to narrow their
wide-eyed wonder,

to fit into this tiny little dot
they *knew*
was not their natural home,

struggling to deny
the warm earthiness
of their wild heart,

the wet fertile land
of their writhing belly,

the mainland,
the heartland,
drifting further away.

They cried for help
in whatever way they could,

but few,
if any,
heard.

Soon they succumbed
like most everyone else,

the fluid body
dismembered,
the i-land made
home.

In denying feeling
they learned to
fit in.

In denying WILL
the dream became real.

BE GENTLE ON YOURSELF

When the still voice of nature
summons you
to begin the steep mountain path

take care not to
forgo your fragile humanity
along the way.

Do not leap out of your skin
and drag its carcass
over brambles and rocks
to meet a mysterious future
you cannot make happen.

Mind any need for the haste of
heroism,
the austere hardened ways
of the past
that may still have words
to deceive you.

Instead,
simply be
gentle on yourself,

walking no further
than where your feet wish to rest
now.

Walk with a patience that
allows for the fervor of living
itself
to unveil the next step,
the next trail on your journey.

Tend to the ordinary,
the simple things
a child would wholeheartedly partake in,

climbing a tree,
skipping over rocks,
making a meal together,
planting a garden,
shaping whispering clouds,
reading to your beloved,
dozing on a bed of kind moss,

the slow caress of your
shaken, neglected body,

a cordial dance under a
broken sky.

Let these tender and
very human moments
be the shrines announcing the
ardency you seek,

the sweet intimacy with all things
needed
to wet the soil
of tomorrow's spring.

II. THE CHILD

INSIDE ME

When my hands and feet
were tender soft
and my eyes
still ripe for the world
there was no distance
between you and I,

the passing cry of an eagle
was felt
as my own,

the blue moon was an
old friend,
its light
touching the light
in my heart,

the melodies of the
crashing ocean
and those of my mother's coos
were waves my
senses ecstatically danced in
the moment they
departed for me,

never a second
separating
my enrapture,

enchanted I was
by this world
I was forever in,

this world
forever inside me.

CLOCKWORK CHILD

The twitching stiff
second hand of the clock
moves swiftly,
brisker than ever,
as anxious children run
circling
round and round,

corralled by confines of
endless diaries
of diurnal drudgery
and detailed doings,
dulling them,

diverting them from
dreams and disorderliness,
devilry

that lie outside
the firm boundaries
of the steel black enclosure,

the edges of this ticker
pushing their red bottoms
forward,

again,
and again,

tapping them onwards

lest they look astray,
wander,
fail somehow,

directing them to the
next number
on this urbane sequentiality,

turning them,
winding them,

readying them
for the Clockwork World.

GROWING DOWN

The same part of you
demanding a child to
grow up
may just be
the one fearful
of growing down,

far down
below the latitudes of thought and order
into deep waters
of the estranged
sinking, feeling body,
the one you once knew
so intimately,

growing down,
planting hands and feet
into the land,

departing synthetic, polished surfaces
for the grim, grit, grass, dirt
the native, untamed part of you
longs to lose itself in,

down,
growing down
into the heart of your beloved child
who enduringly waits for you,

where you can finally
greet her
with moistened eyes,

see in her
a distant you
left behind,

and soften into that
only the heart knows of
where belonging is felt
and life commences.

PLAY IS THE SOIL

Play is the soil
from which a child grows.

Let her flower
naturally,
organically,
and in her own
timing.

Have faith in the soil,
in its minerals and nutrients,
to raise the child
into this world,

have faith in its
creative intelligence
to nurture the qualities immanent
in each newborn child,

the qualities longing to grow
into life.

The quality of *imagination*
that ignites a child
with an array of colors
and perfumes to enchant the world,

of *wonder* and *curiosity* to keep him
opening,
reaching,
unfolding into the mystery
that is life,

of *laughter* to help her
hold herself lightly
as she ascends bravely through
coarse edges of soil and
unrelenting storms,

of *spontaneity* to
devilishly curl his stem,
spot his stigma
and dance his petals
as life inspires him to,

of *flexibility* to
bend her when winds
blow too hard,
and *strength* to
keep her upright,
roots firmly grounded,

of *creativity* to delicately fashion
his seeds and pollen,
and *intuition* to
attune to and work with
that wishing to spread them,

and of *joy*,
the luminous life force that
animates and nourishes her cells,
and fills her senses to overflow
as she sways gloriously
in the Garden of Life.

If only you trust
the nourishment and intelligence
of play
it will feed the child
in ways
you could never conjure.

This does not mean
you stand idly by.

You still need to
water him
and make sure he has
enough sunlight,

ensure he is planted
next to
friendly companions,
and remove harmful critters,

and, of course,
tell him you love him,
often.

But you don't have to
shape the child's bloom
as much as you think
if you simply trust the
subtle, creative, life-giving,
age-old conversation
between play and children
that mysteriously
holds them through
the darkness and delight of
muddy messy times
and guides them upwards
into warm radiance of
brighter days,

from the earthiness of their
spirit
and with the wisdom of
Mother Nature
close to their heart.

You don't have to
pull the child into their
future
if you allow the soil to
do its divinely inherent job –
to birth the seed of potential
into a Cosmos
longing dearly
for its
beauty and fragrance.

SPIRAL WITH ME

Spiral with me
please
turning dust at our feet,
sending it starward
for winds to blow
and galaxies to whirl
far and wide,
to where my daydreaming mind
meets yours.

Let me glimpse into
eternity
with you
spinning with me
as we take detours
upon detours
from the mundane
and mechanical,

trespassing the
thin limen of surety
into the larger part of
ourselves
that rests and kindles us
into full waking moments
the spiral
turns us into.

IN TOUCH

The child is born
to wander unencumbered
through
scattered woods,
to skip over brooks
and boulders,

ecstatically running fingers along
leaves and bark,

gazing intently at
blue angels
doused with splashes
of rain and sunlight.

The child lives to roam free
in unshaped,
undomesticated worlds
belonging to
no one,

senses entrained with the
ensouled livingness
of things,

and in this
he finds belonging,
his rightful place
amongst those things
that breathe and beat and cry
as he does,

unformed and uninformed
yet
by the narrow conveyor belts
of man,

still engaged with
the subtle entreaties
of the forgotten,
of the invisible,

in loving touch
with the undivided center
from which
all arises.

COME OUT AND PLAY

There is something in me
that loves to love,

an insatiable desire
to express,
a longing for life
to flame

through me,
provoking my senses,
turning my eyes white,
writhing my hips,

my lips imbibing
succulently,

my fingers and tongue
purring,
reaching,
sensing
in savage touch,

dancing ecstatically
amongst it all,

the wet soils,
tickling sweet clover,
seducing willows,

as untamed beasts
howl through the night,

and I live
not bound in any way
by shackles of black and white morality,

my wildness
kicked to the corner,
beaten and buried
such that I fit in,
play safe,

be *civilized*,

no,

in no uncertain terms
this burning desire
urges me to be like a child,
shameless,
sucking her luscious thumb,
fondling his ripening self,
screaming to the heavens,
emoting wet and wholly,
naked

while others watch
and leap
from shivering, neglected skin,

and I
burn on
resolutely,
fiercely,
truthfully,
joyously,

thirsty impulses of life
fed through me,
made flesh,
welcomed,

finally,
into my long-captured body,

into the labyrinth of things
under a canopy of wailing stars
that lovingly yearn,
burn
and dream
to come out and play.

III. REFLECTING

A WAVE APPEARS

A wave appears
out of nowhere,

a word,
a phrase,
an image,

a mysterious feeling
rising from the depth
of my belly,

one I know
I must jump on
and ride,

without hesitation,

uncertain of where
it takes me,

following
its mercurial impulse,
the seductive rhythm,

giving way,
not imposing,

allowing it to
wind me through
moment-to-moment
surprise,

another delight,
another twist and turn,

doing what it must,

as seas rise
with excitement,
pulling me closer
into their surging crest,

my heart beating
in ecstatic expression,

my face wet
and heated,

the briny deep feeding me,
eating me alive,

making me its own
untempered doing,

as I fall hard,
deep
into the crescendo
of wild creation.

SOUL PROJECT

There is a quiet witness
that follows me,
watching and wondering
from near and far,

an unceasing gale
blowing discreet kisses in my
inner ear,

while eagerly taking its many notes
on the little things
I choose and not choose,
gathering pieces of wisdom
from my every move,

my leaps and stumbles,
curious about where my
foot plants next,
what road I take in the auspicious
fork ahead,
or how I meet that fateful
shadow
lurking just around the corner,

all the while
devotedly holding the other end of the
invisible thread
that weaves my heart together,

as if I were its endearing
everlasting
soul project, unfolding

as longings dreamt
into orchestrated meanderings
between
brackets of fleeting time,

carried bravely
by this travelling and tiring
vehicle I stand in now
further and further
into far reaches
of the Wild Unknown.

REFUGE

In distraction
we find refuge
from that
longing to find us

it fills us
ever so slightly
as we make way for it

until we turn away
once again
unable to receive another
drip
of its beneficence

our eyes detoured towards
more common pleasures
ones the conditioned mind agrees to

placating opening senses
the cracking heart

our great grandfather's pain
wanting to finally burst through
our skin

the body struggling with
appeal after appeal
it increasingly efforts
to keep at bay

idle chitchat
technology
doing their duty

offering reprieves
from what the body longs for
and is most overwhelmed by.

LIFE'S LONGING

The longing eyes of
darkening clouds
wait
to break
once more,

to pour down
unreservedly,

feeding arid grounds,
cleansing dust
collected on our
feet,

replenishing the thirsty Earth
for those springs
of today
and tomorrow,

for people whose days
have past,

and those rising
in noble cause,

emboldening
tired arms and legs,
strengthening backs
for yet one more day
of heavy travel,

raining joy
into our lives,

arousing a mud twirling,
body unfurling,
ecstatic frenzy,

lifting us higher
into the light
of a beaming sun,

into life's longing
for itself.

COME SIT WITH ME

In a thousand ways
the body asks,

Come sit with me.

To rest in its arms
again
as you once did
so gallantly,
without caution,
without aim,
without a place
to take you away.

Come sit
in this temple of
change,
let yourself feel
its cold waters
pour through you
from one moment to the next,
its textures and grits,
its many hues and prickly bits,
let each place its hand on you
blessing you,
for each comes with a gift,
each is a servant
offering you
another place to sit.

Listen,
if only you listen
to its many ways,
if only you give up
the frays of this existence
to move
into hidden waters of

anger and sadness,
fear and shame,
each creek longing
to take you away,
into streams and rivers
then seas upon seas,
to joyous places
you cannot conceive.

If only
you just drop
the shiny bits
that keep you tracing
this deep descent
and dip your toes
into the waiting river,
sitting,
then submerging
sliver by sliver,
and give yourself back
to what longs to breathe,
to move,
be felt,
and finally set free,
the dark, the light,
the deep unseen,
all you've run from,
all you've been.

WHAT ARE YOU BRINGING?

Comfortably I sit
on a heaping mound of snow,
pale backdrop,
frosty full mist in the air.

Tucking my heavy backpack aside,
I suddenly hear the joy
and collegial murmurings
of a distant group.

Bursts of laughter
intertwine themselves charmingly
amidst fervent conversation,
delighting my ears,
wing me.

Yet with each passing moment
a pang in my chest takes residence,
a heartbreak,
a loneliness,
a longing for more.

To my surprise
a voice calls to me,

"What are you bringing?"

Hurriedly I remove my glove,
reach into my backpack,
pull out a piece of paper and pen,
and write, of course,

Strength.

Jagged branches of lightening
dart beneath me,
gnashing,

as the mound collapses
by a foot.

Swift fear places my hands down
to sturdy,
eyes fleeting,
another deep pang in my chest.

Immediately, they call out again,
but with more thrust,

"What are you bringing?!"

Once more I reach,
this time with greater urgency,
pulling out another piece of paper
from my sodden backpack,
and after a brief pause, I write again,

Strength!

The mound crackles and moans,
shifting, breaking even more.

My heart pounds
sharply,
spreading
ominously,
plumes of breath
rising rapidly.

For a moment,
the still silence of
only winter days
permeates the crisp air
of my unease,

offering itself
to my grinding chest.

I decide to pack up and leave
but then the distant voice
travels the icy mist once more
but with a new sense of
calm urgency,
an assertive appeal for something more,
as if conferring a final call,
a summoning of something
I doubt I can find.

"What are you bringing?!"

Another piece of paper
is quickly placed on my lap.
I pause, pensively,
my hand trembling,
my chest unbearable,
and with pen in hand,
I stubbornly write,

Strength!!

The sweeping raven kraas,
the towering cedars shudder,
and the once sturdy snowy hill
bellows its final call,
a chilled woeful cry.

It collapses and opens,
tumbling, falling down
as it consumes me
deep into the abyss of its
yawning icy core.

Buried, trapped
in its frozen embers,
an ineffable fear takes hold.

I scream for the Gods.

And then awake.

DARK ROOM

The dark room you
continue to fill
may soon burst.

Another restless thought
and thing deemed
essential
crowds suffocating spaces.

Rearranging couches and armoires
and polishing prized silverware
to glint
doesn't seem to help.

A remedial orderliness,
an ostensible ornateness,
a coming together of minds
for one more clever stratagem

and still
your knee gashes against the
cluttered desk,

and you trip once more
onto the
the waiting bed,

your loneliness cloaked
in the dim of
well-trained anxiety,

forgetful
of the one thing you long for,
the only thing
that illumines the eyes.

THE JUGGLER

The wise juggler
tosses beliefs high in the air
one after another
under the luminescent sky,

holding on,
but for only a moment,

knowing that what lay in hand
is not *it*,
is not Truth,
but merely perspective.

Thoughts position themselves
anew
tirelessly filling empty space,

but again,
humbly, they are released,
hands remaining open
like the muted azure above,

receptive
to that elusive something
that can only arrive
if made room for.

Breathing in
then breathing out

the juggler waves his hands
bereft
of secondhand stories,
divisive conclusions,
and filters of conjecture,

opening to wrong
when right takes residence,
considerate of good
when bad plants itself,

transcending both
in a rhythm bearing
the wide lens of contradiction,

knowing
that in grasping too long
paradigms crash,

worlds fragment
onto the patient ground,

the force of gravity
doing its work,

assisting,

making space
for the Great Mystery
to find the juggler once more
from beyond the confines of thought,

until grasped again.

PRAYER

You send your prayers
to the moon and stars,
but are you willing to live them
today?

You seek,
but are you willing to
find,

to open your arms
wide enough
to cradle your dreams,

to sing the songs
long reined by your
shallow breath?

Send your prayers,
but first pray to
open and receive,

to wash away the old film
cluttering your view,

to unveil yourself
to the pathways
calling for your footprints.

Pray for the harvest,
but first prepare the inner soil
to be planted,

prepare yourself to live the
unlived life,

the one you want
and desperately fear
at the same time.

TRICKSTER MEDICINE

You are there,
you have made it,
finally,
you have what you want.

Or do you?

Just as the hand
claims its
long awaited prey,
along comes the
Trickster
to take it
away.

The punchy new manager
shatters the glass
cubicle
you so dedicate yourself to.

Injuries buckle you to the
sidelines
to hear,
feel,
what you keep running from.

Your beloved breaks
the sealed box
you both comfortably sit on
and dare not look into.

An arid financial spell
forces you to a
humble watering hole
to quench a deeper thirst.

All soups
need to be stirred.

The Trickster
holds the spoon.

Paint chips,
windows crack,
pipes burst,
and money lacks.

You win
you lose,
bodies glisten
and they age,
slowing you,
humbling you,
well-thought plans
shatter,
polished bubbles of success
burst,
troubling you,
unsteadying you,
prison walls of perceived security
dissolve,
weakening you,
redirecting you
to so much more,
reminding you,
that none of it
was what you wanted
anyways.

The quiet whisperer
in you
yearns to melt into
deep golden seas,
not ride atop
ephemeral waves
skimming along this world.

It longs to
break your flaming heart
wide open,
burning beliefs,
ambitions,
and dreams,
ideas
of who you are
and what should be,

away
in an ancient fire
lovingly lit by the
wily Coyote,
a sober ritual
of thankfulness to
his countless emissaries
working in service
of the unsteadying force of
change.

SUFFERING IS THE GATEWAY

Suffering is the gateway
for that
which you long for most.

Be grateful when it arrives.

It may be your best chance.

WHAT AM I SAYING YES TO?

What am I saying Yes to?

Am I saying *Yes* to the
music coming from my
ear buds
or from the birds whose songs
ring eternally?

Am I saying *Yes* to
reaching for my phone
one more time,
or to taking in the warm smiles
and kind gestures
of strangers
passing by?

What else might I notice
if I create room for the
sweetness of here and now?

What else might
reach me?

Again, I ask myself,

What am I saying Yes to?

Am I saying *Yes* to the job
that's never fed my soul,
that belongs in the box
so many others accept
as their own?

Do I continue to choose to
dry up in its ceaseless demands,
to become sterile,
empty of life?

Or am I willing to take the risk
to say a hardy *Yes*
to the hum's and ha's of my
forgotten imagination,
of the forgotten child within,

to leap
from the edges of my cluttered desk
and open myself
wide
to what could be,

to adventure,
to aliveness only found
in the spiraling winds of
unpredictability?

What am I saying Yes to?

Am I saying *Yes* to the
storms of anxious thought
I wake to every morning
and take so literally,
the ones that fail to forecast my life
time and again?

Or do I pause long enough
and breathe deep enough
to create room for an inner *Yes* to
arise and confirm that
everything is and will be okay,
unfolding just as it should?

What am I saying Yes to?

Am I saying *Yes* to

spending time with
this person
and that person,

with those who, once again,
fall short of stoking the fires
of my heart?

Am I saying *Yes* to
spreading my energy
around the block
for all to take?

Or do I say *Yes* to
walking away from those
who do not feed me,
to claiming and enlarging the
pockets of space
I've so routinely filled?

What am I saying Yes to?

How am I spending these
precious moments,
the urgency of this precious time
I feel I am running out of
as days, months and years
seem to fly by
before me
faster and faster,

as this beautiful existence
I am learning to love
so much
slips
from my grasp,

fades
before my eyes?

What am I reading?
What am I watching?
What am I exposing myself to?

How am I enjoying each of these
dying moments,
these dying people,
the ones I cherish more deeply
each passing day,
the ones I cannot help but
hold tighter to?

What am I saying Yes to
here, now,

as I sit before this
mysterious person,
this miracle of life?

Am I saying *Yes* to the
trivial agendas in my mind,
the flurry of judgments,
the tireless, divisive thoughts
claiming to have *the* answer,

those thoughts that want to take me
far away,
anywhere
but here
with her?

Or am I saying *Yes* to

giving myself over
to her,
this sacred woman,

to this one
miraculous moment in time
together,
never to be repeated?

What am I saying Yes to?

As soon as I say *Yes* to one thing
I say *No* to another.

One door opens
and another closes.

It closes, perhaps, to what I
truly want.

I shut the door
sending ripples of intent
across the sea of life,

declaring I am
saying *No* to a deeper hunger,
an old itch,
to joy,

and saying *Yes* to this
same old tiring story,

declaring that this pain
is what I deserve,
and that onus
is what I value,

that this reality
is what I choose to live in

when really,
it is not what I want
at all,

and yet somehow,
for some reason,
I still say *Yes* to it,

again and again.

I keep saying *Yes*
in these dying days,
in these dying moments
of my one and only
precious life.

I must therefore ask myself
again,

What am I saying Yes to?

Am I saying *Yes* to
taking the risk to be
transparent,

vulnerable to the voice that
wants to be
heard,

to the feelings that
want to be
felt,

to speaking the words that have wanted to
scream
from below and above
for decades,
for millennia?

Or am I staying shut,
saying *Yes* to playing the
game of hiding out,
tortured in my
incubated existence,

silently crying the tears of those
before me
who never had the chance
to safely speak their truth,
to stand firm in their integrity?

What am I saying Yes to?

Am I saying *Yes* to
wearing the fabrics
I have so devoutly worn for others,
the shabby frayed threads
handed down through the
generations?

Or am I willing to
tear them off,
stand naked,
alone
in my own tender belonging,
in the place of wonder
I lost
lifetimes ago?

What am I saying Yes to?

How many ways can I
fully live this moment,
welcome life into my senses?

How many ways can I
sing the dying song that
wants to be sung,

live this fading longing
desperately wanting to take shape
in my life?

How many ways can I
love the little moments,
smile at them,
turn each into a warmth,
a joy,
I can rest into?

How many ways can I
savor this beating heart,
this breath of yours
and mine?

Upon my deathbed
how can I know
that I held life
close to my chest,

that I leaned into this precious existence
and gave myself over
to its beauty
we are ever graced with?

Indeed,
the question begs to be asked
again and again,

What am I saying Yes to?

BEFRIEND YOUR DOUBTS

Befriend your doubts,

they exist
for good reason.

They see chinks
in surfaces
others
blindly turn from
in the castle of crumbling knowledge
most
make their home,

each doubt
casting questions
at its exalted walls
others dare not ask,

widening fissures
set
by those brave ones
before
who risked breaking
the spell of certitude
and servitude,

who could not ignore
the faint soundscape
humming through the cracks
dimming noise
most resign themselves to,

who sensed
venerable shapes
speaking
from the other side
begging to reclaim
their form,

each doubt
inviting light
into the shadows,

dismantling
long cherished walls,

fading the line
between old friends,

uniting worlds upon worlds.

UNTIL I'M READY

I let myself need
until I can stand alone.

I let myself hold on
until my fingers let go.

I let myself stay frozen
until ready to thaw.

I let myself remain rigid
until ready to tremble.

I let myself be silent
until ready to speak.

I let myself doubt
until ready to believe.

I let myself remain closed,
hidden,
until ready to open,
be seen,

ready to hear that question,
feel that answer.

Gingerly,
inch by inch,
I let myself crawl
until ready to walk,
walk
until ready to run,
run
until ready to leap,
leap
until ready to
soar with the stars.

I let myself stay here,
still,
in these old familiar aches
until ready to return
to whence they came.

These old stories
get to remain sealed
until I'm ready to release them
back into the Earth.

Gently,
compassionately,
I give myself over
to exactly where I am,
to this tender familiar place
for as long as it's needed,

until I'm ready,

until something deep within
stirs me to move
from this sacred ground
that has held me,
carried me,
served me
so well.

FREEDOM

The demon in your
mind,
the perverseness
twisting in your
belly,
the rage seizing you
day and night,

it may be prudent
to incarcerate this
serious offender
at first,

placing it in a cage,
locked away,
safely removed
from you.

But eventually
it would be wise
to courageously
walk into that
shadowy room
bearing candlelight,

and peer
into its
fearful,
savage eyes,

standing strong
as you must,
even as it violently
shakes its cage,
hissing at you,
spitting profanities,
desperately reaching out
through the steel bars

trying to possess you
just one more time.

It would behoove you to
study this
insidious monster,
this
creature of darkness,
to get to know it,
and understand its
reasoning and ways.

And over time
if trust is gained
you may find yourself
befriending it,

and then feeling called
to open its cage wide,
ending this apartheid
of us and them,
this warring and enmity,

for in keeping it
imprisoned
you stand in prison
with it,

in fearing it,
fear still lives in you.

And then
as time passes,
and you strengthen
your bridge of
mutual trust
and kinship,

you may choose to
couple with it
as allies,
it your wise teacher
of the night,

for it has much
to share,
much to reveal
about the dark forces
haunting this world.

In its kind and generous
darkness
your candle only stands
to shine brighter.

And finally
when you have traveled
at great length with
each other,
and any last remnants
of distance between you
have dissolved,

naturally
you will find yourself
pulling this presence
deep into your heart,

united
at long last
with your
dear beloved.

HOW WELL DO YOU BOW?

How well do you bow?

How well do you allow your
steeled body to
melt into suppleness,

to yield as day fades to night,
fold like dream-bound hibiscus petals,
fall like rainbow leaves of Autumn,

to become lissome
like a child,

responsive to life's mercurial mischief,
its sinuous dialect
only a child can speak?

How well do you let
gravity do its work,
tilting you,
pulling your head
down
closer to your heart
where wordless words
announce themselves,

away from your
plumb high-rise,
the tiring routes
lining your mind
keeping you upright
and up-tight,

growing down,
acquiescing you
towards something
far more quiet,
far more real,

something long desiring to
loosen you
into what the Plant Nation
holds secret,

as sensed behind the still,
captivating eyes
of the Animal Kingdom,

as felt in fresh Waters
yearning to wash you clean
of all accumulated trivialities,
all concrete lanes and straight up lies
deceiving you from entering
the fluid stream of life,

from bowing deeper

into the coaxing
Earth
eager to see your lined face,

to break you asunder
and scatter you
far afield
burying you,
seeding you,

such that you rise anew,
an offering to the Heavens
and Earth,

undulating,
meandrous,
feral,

your long-awaited
reclamation,

living as life
intended you to,

bowed to the sacred,
your empty, wild
home.

BIRDSONG

Listen deeply

and you may hear
the birdsong
greeting you
early morning
as having a message

just for you.

IV. RELATING

DANCE OF PARADOX

Loosening ourselves
from the
tug of war we are in

we remember

we are simply
pulling ourselves
into each other
bit by bit,

unraveling, spiraling,

into nothing
and everything

at the same time.

INTO THE SEA

There was a time
when my love
was unrequited,
and enduring heartbreak
left me for loss,
away from our
expected kinship and belonging,
setting me sail
across stormy seas of longing
and despair.

There was a time
when I blamed you
for my departure,
for having to drift
in darkness away from the
hands whose touch I
trusted,
but could trust no more.

The clouds above
drifting from
shores behind
would not leave my
wake,
carrying reminders
of waters not yet
felt,
and shrouded beams of brightness
not yet known.

The stormy seas
only billowed more
as I refused to look up
and acknowledge the
shadows that fell
upon me,

the ones that
severed me from
my past,
my one true love.

They rocked
the sturdiness
I determinedly crafted,
sought to maintain,
and thought mine to keep,
the drifting direction
I staunchly came to believe in.

And the boat groaned beneath me
even more.

The sails, working hard
on behalf of my
gritted narrow push,
soon tired,
cracks breaking through
their stretched fading linen,
spreading themselves
across the face of
my thrust.

Lightening struck
the battered mast in half,
and the deluge from
the inescapable overcast
poured itself,
filling the one thing
I could call my own,
the only thing
I had left.

The wooden frame
shook what little ground
I had,
splinting
breaking,
rotting,
the raging sea,
beckoning.

I clung
to its sinking ways,
clung to the only
dream I had,
clung hopelessly watching it,
my life,
fall apart
again,
piece by piece,
torturously,
the gaping mouth of the ocean
widening,
willfully demanding
to take me
and swallow me whole,
into a remembrance
I unknowingly
came to find.

ONE SONG

It seems the whole of life
is conspiring in my favor,

slowly singing me awake
in this living theatre,

some roaring anthems,
some subtle chants,
some cheery melodies,
some consoling croons,

a chorus of notes
sung seemingly separate,

a symphony of One
sung through many

braving on
in harmonious union.

WINK OF STARLIGHT

Courageously
we continue to travel
into the unknown of
each other's hearts,
carrying on
despite it all.

Through sticky dark patches
we persevere,
lifting one foot
after another
out of old mud
that follows our feet.

Through rising mists
appearing as dead ends
somehow
a faint light is seen
peaking through at us,
calling us to brave on.

Each challenge
another invitation
to travel further along this
winding path
from my heart
to yours,
closer,
our faithful companions
offering themselves
each step of the way.

The faint giggles
cheering us
through messy mire,
the blazing stars
winking
through dim fog,

we are held
from beyond the edges
of time,
bestowed with hopeful nudges
and reminders
of this sacred pilgrimage
we agreed to walk
long before
our eyes ever met.

FOUND

There are those who wish
you to stay tried and torn,
tightly sealed in your
tattered hand-me-down hut
where all the masses find you
and feed you
tables full of falsehood and trivialities,
of who you are not,

but rare is the one
who sees in you
hidden acquiescence
aching in your chest,
the beating that's
dulled and made way
for the liking of others
but that still quietly
cries hope,
cries for its freedom,

a hiddenness we sense
in the pause of the butterfly,
in the starlight twinkle of a
child's eyes,
in the ensouling stillness
of dawn
when all disappears
but our love making,

in these sweet, eternal spaces
that humbly shape the
quiet background of living,
that we only see
from the corner of our eyes,
do we long to be found.

ALIVE

Glass home
tautly decorated
grey customs
and prints
tolerated,
drifting thoughts
as time goes by
hoping for something
not knowing
what or why,
if only when
comes
that special guest
filling what's empty
your waiting unrest,
silent cries
hidden in disguise
not a whisper of
truth
one can find,
idle chatter
a glancing eye
promising glimmer
another good-bye,
safely sealed
your knowing heart
the undreamt dreams
the unlived love,
not known of
under ceilings high
forever waiting
held by
your design,
getting by
only bit by bit
meal after meal
another news clip,

you go on
in fragile glass home
surrounded by many
yet feeling alone,
ceilings crack
and windows break
welcoming in
that fateful day,
a stone is thrown
from just outside
a dear old friend
breaking you alive.

LEND A HAND

Endlessly we climb this
diverging ladder,
one with no top
or bottom,
reaching
for the next rung
as best we know how
in our unique way and timing,

stretching
like the unfurling fern frond
towards courting sunlight,
or the potted plant
that longs
through the thin window pane
for glimpses
of something more.

It is an age-old longing
to reach for a distant star
and sit in its perch
resting
until stirred upwards
to the next,
and next,
each star
a broader vista,
a cradling light
to warm ourselves into.

It is the ancient pilgrimage,
a mythic story carried by the wind
and sung by crackling fires,
one toted by the
drum beat of ants,
gorging worms,
soaring salmon,

and of the
swifts, swallows and finches
sailing through naked skies.

It is the child
who hungers to stand,
then walk,
and soon run
further into vivid fields
of imagination,
and the mother who
lifts him,
this bundle of wonder,
joyfully
upwards
into the heavens
for angels to behold.

It is the longing
of our hearts
to feast at generous tables
not yet laid,
to travel through
far-flung magical kingdoms,
and drink
from the grail of
holy wisdom
descending from
old fabled moonlight.

And it is our
great collective longing
not just for ourselves,
but for others as well,
for this soulful family
we are forever bonded to,
to lend a hand,

make it available
for others to reach
and hold,
and to lift them
into more tender meadows.

Yet, all we can do
on this journey
is lend a loving hand,

offer it
so those before us have the
choice
to reach for something
more.

In reaching down
they can reach up.

It is our gift,
our purpose,
our greatest joy.

We cannot force our hand
into theirs,
nor can we serve
with a hand shaped
for certain desired arrangements.

We serve when our hand is
steady
for those hands that tremor,
firm
for those that clutch,
soft
for those that are raw.

We serve
when our hand carries within it
the promise of a
broken heart,

when it emanates
compassion to the one that
asks,
that aches,

that is ready to
reach
for something hitherto
not known of
within darkness of
days past.

We serve
by kindly offering to carry their
weighty bag,
in lending our ear
to their fledgling dreams,
by sharing our ticklish smile
with their restless child,
and in giving warm presence
to their cold sorrow.

We serve
by the little things we do,

but mostly,
by demonstrating
a new way,

and by seeing in them
a truth and beauty

beyond the
fear and shame
they have long
shaped themselves with.

We lend a hand
by being the kindred
Nature
that recognizes itself
in another.

You are that
One.

You are that
gateway.

You are that
radiant star
to so much more.

IN HARMONY

The tug
of yours and mine,

the push and pull
of wistful desire,

in compromise
we stay separated,
hidden treasures
inside,

with hearts opening
we meet in time,

our truth burning
as one fire,

two songbirds
singing
whose songs
harmonize.

Can we wait
long enough
to find that
meadow
where we stand
joyfully,

stars coalescing our
dreams,
sowing them
into the earth
walked upon together?

Can we be
patient enough
for the mystery

to unify the
eagle and swan,
the sky and earth,

to weave us deeply into
the horizon
where all things
emerge from,
to hear,
to sing
our one beloved song?

ONE LAST TIME

I sit
facing you,
hands folded neatly
in my lap,
conversation
flowing well
as it so often has,
one last chorus to share
together
in this
old familiar world
we've danced
so many steps in,
one last look
at the dusty pictures
on the wall
I framed
and hung
one stormy night
that feels like yesterday,
one last sip
from the beige mug
I always drink
my morning coffee from
while seated
on the
threadbare sunken side of the couch
looking at you,
now,
lips whispering,
fingers longing
for just
one last touch,
eyes
holding on,
caught in tender
silence
with you,

here
again,
one last time,
afraid
of what will happen
when I leave,
of where life will take me
when I walk out that
old familiar door.

NEW CONSTELLATION

As I began to drink from the
well of deep sorrow
its waters rippled outward
in all directions,
further than I could conceive,

touching those dearest to me,
in particular,

the warm undulations
mysteriously finding them,
irrigating their thirsty senses,

turning them ever so slightly
towards one another
in new constellation,
new conversation,

towards the well of
deep sorrow
they long to drink
from.

MYSTERIOUS UNFOLDING

I sit
gazing at those before me,
the many shapes, sizes
colors and backgrounds,
feeling,
more than ever,
the mystery we are unfolding in
together,
seemingly separate,
yet united at once.

I sink
further into a feeling
that I cannot possibly
know who
this multitude of beings is,

the roads they travel,
the fine wisdom they are here
to gather,
the dark caves calling their name,

the pain and grief they must carry,
the unsung longing in their hearts,
the deep complexity of their
timeless nature,

my conclusions
ostensible at best,

my judgments
a reflection,

my desire to help
well-intended.

My heart breaks open
further,

softening me,
humbling me,

as I realize
I am not in control
as much as I think,

for each courageous soul
unfolds within
and beyond time
in ways my mind
cannot fathom,

a dream of creation
held and guided
by a timelessness
I've only just begun
melting into.

STEEPENING ASCENT

The ascent
only gets steeper
and more rigorous
as we close in
on the peak,

the bitter alpine
doing all
to prevent us from climbing
a step further,

the tenacious frost
biting our lips,
numbing our senses,

gaping crevices
enticing us into their
hungry bellies,

seemingly
sturdy snow packs
breaking apart,
crumbling down,

as angry headwinds
determinedly announce themselves,
commanding us to leave
forthwith,

to not trespass
one more inch,
ending this futile quest,

admonishing us
to set up camp,
that this is as good as
it's going to get,

or to find another
more suitable mountain
altogether.

Still,
something spurs us
onwards,

stubbornness perhaps,
or maybe we're just
hard on ourselves,
or we simply remember
all we've been through
to get here.

Yet, it's
more than that,
it feels,

a slight something
that finds us
amongst the grim
and blinding blizzards,

a faithful echo,
faint and somehow familiar,
rising from the
silent blue abyss,

urging us
to battle through the elements
one more day,
step after mighty step,
past the mounting refusals,
over an ever-hardening,
crusty
surface,

through the thin
cloud ceiling

to the apex
of our one
tender heart.

SHE IS THE DOOR

She is the door.

She won't let you in
until
you surrender to her,
until
you set down
the tattered old baggage
you have carried
and worshipped
these many years.

Drop the illusions
of your mind,
the ideas
of who you are:
the bluster,
the charm,
the false pretense,
the wild, well-versed stories
you tell so well.

The ones you have
deceived
so many others with.

None will work with her,
her piercing eyes see
right through them.

None will be the key
that opens the door,
that opens her heart.

Leave them at the threshold,
let them slip from your hand
and fall crashing to the floor,

leaving you
naked,
empty,
vulnerable,

leaving you
seen.

Only then can you be received.
Only then can you enter
the sacred gateway.

There is a dream you have lived
that is no longer yours
to keep,
a dream that has carried you
and served you well,
an alluring dream
from which you are now waking.

Something magnificent,
something ineffable
waits for you
on the other side.

Something new
wants to be born.

Only what is real
can cross through.

Only what is real
can remain.

Everything else
must fall away.

FIRE OF UNITY

Each time we give ourselves
over to each other
another part of us dies,
offered to the fire of
unity,

each piece
necessary
for the fire to burn
brighter,

to the heavens
and back,

a sacrifice
to our indivisible source
that longs for our
sacred return
to places
only the fire
can take us.

EYE TO EYE

There is in me
you

we see
eye to eye.

~

A break from wild empty spaces
to acknowledge and appreciate
that which fills them.

THE LITTLE THINGS

Amongst the busyness of life
there lies innumerable moments
to pause,
take in,
and appreciate
the many little things
we so easily take for granted.

The precise crafting
of your wooden chair
and how it
dedicatedly offers you
a place to sit and rest,

the soft warmth
of your pillow
easing you into sleep
every night,

the laundry basket
neatly holding all your clothes
together,
keeping your home
a little bit more tidy,

the sweet cinnamon smell
of baked goods
steaming from your
steadfast oven,
the one that
works hard to cook for you,
ensuring your body is
nourished with heated
fare.

The lure of greener pastures
is quite tempting,

but there are so many
sights to behold,
so many textures
and tastes to savor
and give thanks to
right here and now
in everyday living,

if only we pause our
fleeting thoughts,
and flittering eyes
long enough
to take them in.

The door handle
that enables you to
safely secure your home,
giving you assurance
and peace of mind
every time you leave,

the thoughtfully designed
bronze picture frame
that faithfully
stores and shares
that golden moment
by the lake with your family,
a moment it helps you
to never forget,

the electrical socket
carefully installed,
allowing you to have light
to read your favorite book with,
the one
tightly bound for your
nightly imaginings.

There are
an infinite number of reasons
to be grateful
for the little ways
life is made simpler,
safer
and more enjoyable.

I am thankful
for the farmer
who grows the colorful food
I feed myself with,
and for the
truck driver
who commutes long hours
to deliver it to the grocery store
up the road.

I am thankful
for the skilled mechanic
who tends to my car
so I can safely drive towards the
spacious alpine
to care for my health and spirit,
tent neatly packed,
the one carefully sealed
to keep me dry.

I am thankful for
the curtains draping my windows,
for each hard earned thread
sewn
that offers me
the privacy and comfort
I need
to make my home
feel like home.

I am grateful
for each unsung hand
that has touched me
in some way,
both those that I have
held and seen
and those
working in the distance,
inconspicuously tending to the little things
we so easily forget
and take for granted,
those little things
that when added up
form the fine web of
human existence
we partake in.

~

V. SLOWING

COMPASSIONATE RESTRAINT

Stay still,
non-ambitious
for a while,
listening for something
that longs to find you
in your heartbreak
and rare moment of pause.

This is not a time to
push as you have,
to travel familiar routes.

This is a time to be
graced
by a light
only found
in the still point of
darkness,

by subtle words
only heard
in pause,

when you no longer have eyes
for the next trail
and every step leads to
further stumble,

the shackles of submission
tightening
with each struggle,
holding you in
compassionate restraint.

Alas, this is the moment
for your deepest exhale,
one you have been waiting for,

a moment when the skies are
clear and dark enough
for you to finally
see the stars.

WHEN YOU SLOW DOWN ENOUGH

When you slow down enough
you no longer fear
the silence of space
and all it holds.

In embracing stillness
you discover that
which you never knew existed
or was possible,
and you meet
your Self
and life
perhaps
for the
very first time.

When you slow down enough
you finally
feel the feelings
and
hear the words
you have been avoiding
all these many years.

Those knocks on the door,
those peering eyes that
have been trying to
capture your attention
from the shadows,

the long lost dream
that once carried you away,
far away,
many moons ago.

When you slow down enough
you no longer fear
your aloneness.

You reflect on how
distractions
have conveniently kept you,
and others,
from the spaciousness
of the Self.

You understand how
lonely one can feel
in a crowded room
full of family and friends,
and how connected
one can feel
in the clear simplicity of
solitude.

When you slow down enough
you make it okay to say
No to others
so that you can say
Yes to You.

You love yourself enough
to make self-care a priority,
even if those around you
question why you are suddenly
less available,

even if your
guilty
pleasing
responsible mind
kicks and screams,
fearful you may
offend,
fearful you may
let someone down.

When you slow down enough
infinite treasures of
divine imagination
begin to fill
your heart and mind.

The fire of creativity speaks
through you
and *consumes* you
with joyful, playful delight!

Suddenly,
you are led along
unforeseen
artistic adventures,
your hand,
your brush,
your hammer,
taken,
and you are pulled into the
dance of co-creation,
into a new sense of
meaning and
purpose.

When you slow down enough
you make this moment enough.

You hear,
truly hear,
the soft pattering of rain drops
on the sidewalk.

You stop to take in the
strength and presence
of our magnificent trees

and stand in awe
at how they
majestically reach
for the skies.

You lose yourself
in a colorful bug,
just as you did
when you were a child.

You sit quietly on a log
with your eyes closed,
just you,
your breath,
and the air
caressing your skin.

This moment
when you make it enough
becomes a
long lost dear friend
that never left your side
that you
recognize and include
and appreciate
once again.

When you slow down enough
you let yourself be enough.

You release your firm grip
from your To-Do's,
to settle into the softness
of your To-Be's,

to muse with wonder
at what it is to be
a human being
living on this
green and blue orb
traveling
the Great Mystery
we call life,

to feel yourself
come home
back into your heart,
finally,
resting in the place
you have been circling,
the place
you have been searching for
all along.

WHISPERING WORDS

I run to greet my
father,
eager to teach him
everything I've discovered
about myself
and life,

to sway him
to the other side,
to me,
to who I think
he should be.

As I enter the
busy bus terminal
an old melody
graces me
from the ceiling speakers,

as if reaching
into the
well of my existence,
long past my ears,

singing to and stilling me
between ticks
of clock-time.

Let It Be

says these whispering words,
inviting momentary reflective pause,

a sudden forgo
of my
well-intentioned and impassioned
agenda,

heartening me to
let my father
be
just as he is

now,

standing before me
proudly
in his crisp striped suit,
bright yellow tie
and
shiny leather briefcase,

these timely words
swaying me to
simply
walk beside him
in his hard-won and
seasoned stride.

Later that evening
I seek quiet in the seclusion
of Mother Nature,

sitting reflectively
on a long damp log
in a spacious grove

guarded by the luring presence of
ancient Cedar and Pine trees,
a full moon gazing down,
cascading its warm light
upon me,

when suddenly
a wise elder approaches.

With an air of
sublime strength
she stands tall
directly in front of me
like one of the great trees
herself,

and looks fiercely
into my eyes,
piercing me
from a depth of worlds
not known of.

She imparts many pieces of
sage wisdom,
but only one is
remembered from this
auspicious night.

She whispers...

*There is only so much
you can do for others.*

*Let Oneness
take care of the rest.*

TRUST THOSE EMPTY SPACES

You do not need to
carry it all
for everyone,
nor deliver it
on a solid silver platter.

You do not need to
bring every detail
in every form,
filling every crack
and every pause.

You do not need to
fix the strains and pains,
stabilizing what longs to
fall apart
and break open.

Trust those empty spaces,
the unclosed wounds
you may be tempted to patch up
and make better.

Trust those empty spaces,
the unplanned plans,
the routes that exist on the
other side of the map.

Trust those empty spaces,
the unthought thoughts
that desire to emerge
naturally,
and without your fashioning.

Trust those empty spaces,
the eleventh hour
when still
no one is knocking at your door.

Trust those empty spaces,
the times of great loss,
when the high dreams of tomorrow
are all but gone.

Trust those empty spaces,
when you finally say *No*
to picking up the pieces
others have dropped.

Trust those empty spaces,
the moment you cannot walk another mile
in shoes
others expect you to wear.

Trust those empty spaces,
when you offer your hand
and for the first time
it is not received.

Trust those empty spaces,
when you crumple over,
shattering ways
you've long held yourself together.

Trust those empty times,
those moments of despair
and confusion,
when you cannot find your path
nor help others
find their own.

Trust the invisible hand
to reach you
in the eleventh hour,
in the moment of release,

when all can no longer be
carried,
and all is but
gone.

Trust the space between,
making room for the mystery
to do its work for you,
to emerge,
filling in cracks
of your breaking heart,
tending to you,
finding you,
in its myriad of ways
when time.

RED LIGHT

I drive us
to our next destination.

Amidst the flurry
of conversation
with my beloved
beside me
I pause
at that red light,
look over,
and in the authenticity of silence
offer a tender smile
and caress her
cool cheek.

We meet
if only for a few moments,
for as long as that
red light will allow,

we find one another
again,

in-between it all,
the busy traffic,
the breathless words,
the endless tasks,

we reach across
that busy intersection
and remember

that what we long for,
and hope this
winding road will lead us to,

lies here
all along,

where we sit now

at this red light.

DESIGNED TO DISAPPOINT

The life I live
is designed to disappoint,

a crushing meadow of
hopes and dreams,

my skin loosening
its faithful brace,

my beloved slowly
departing
into darker days of twilight,

like silky wet moss
drying to dust,

and the beaver's den
seized by the fierce
river of time,

leaving me lost
and found
in a sea of wild grace,

taken
by that which
never surrenders
to hold me closer.

BACK TO LIFE

Forgotten are those
quiet moments
when suddenly
you disappear
and there is nothing left
but the thrumming
of the river
that finds you
in this space you have
finally given yourself
over to,

when nothing matters
except this timelessness
you dwell in
that envelopes you
in its arms
and makes you
its own

as one with the forest
and the beating raindrops
and the mysterious sounds
from winged friends
passing by
all welcoming you
back to life.

Oh dear one,
this is your sacred moment
of coming home to your
senses,
to yourself,
the wild kingdom
you are.

SUDDENLY I DON'T KNOW

Suddenly I don't know,
another piece of certainty
crumbles away,
my heart breaking open.

Another loss,
another window of
longstanding views
cracked,
another dam broken
in the river of truth.

Each time I stumble,
pushed further to my knees,
down, closer to the quiet of
Mother Earth

calling me to lay
in her strong arms
empty of all
beginnings and endings
taken by time,

inviting me to gaze upwards
into the eternal black,

baptized
into the nameless space
my soul longs to
dwell in.

RESTING IN THE GARDEN OF LOVE

Are you willing to rest
in the
Garden of Love?

Are you willing to
lay down your tools
and maps
for a moment
and give yourself over
to its moist earth
beneath your feet?

Are you willing to
take in its mist
enveloping the dark green forests
rising upwards into the sky,
and its soft sway of lime lace branches
running finger tips
over silvery streams?

Are you willing to
give yourself over to its
mottled ladybug wings
tickling hairs on your arm,
and its drifting candles
flickering through
dark seas above?

Are you willing to
let your heart break open
to its piercing gaze
and serenaded melodies
cast from the innocence of
young children?

Can you feel it?
Can you hear it
singing you home?

You speak of great love,
but can you
offer enough space
between your words
for its ancient language
to speak to you?

You read many books
on its wisdom,
but can you be still enough
to hear
its guiding whispers
between the lines?

You travel many distances
searching for its promise,
but can you end your circling
long enough
to plant yourself
into its fecund fields,
and softly sway
from its leafy branch?

You try to be its emissary
with your profound words,
but can you simply rest
with another
in the Garden of tender listening
and warm empathy,
and have that
be enough?

You produce great acts of
service,
but can you sink into
the Garden's shady spaces
long enough to

soften the rough edges
of your past?

Can you faithfully sit
at Love's hearth
while its heated embers
thaw ice-captured stories
of yesteryear?

Are you willing?

Where do you think you are
trying to get to
in this mysterious life?

Do you really know
where you are going
and what you truly want?

Have you not heard
the lullaby of birds
reminding you of an
old song
you used to sing?

Have you not felt
the primordial hum of stone
calling you
through the core of your
bones?

If only you rest
in the space between
all you seek
and all you know,

in the lush wilderness
of doubt and uncertainty,
you will find it there
waiting,
patiently,
as all you've ever
wanted,
as the Garden
you've longed to
return to.

VI. RETURNING

TURNING

You left me
when desire could no longer
contain itself
and leaped at the chance

so my hand released yours
and adventure took you
to the other side

where the light fades
and you believe this
to be life

my hand
still open
awaiting your unrest

when you can
no longer be with
life as you see it

when troubled times
lead you to question
to doubt

when you dare listen to the
faintest of longing

that which
never leaves you

your heartbreak growing stronger
with each moment of devout
attention

slowly turning you away
back
towards me

towards that which only the
deepest part of you
can touch

and which makes you
alive.

DREAMS

The dream I carried
for years
lay tightly sealed
in my fist

until frightened fatigued fingers
finally gave way,
pried open by the jags
of time,

the dream fast asleep,
cradled in my unfolding hand

lay bare now
to hungry beams of fresh sunlight
rushing in,
warming and stirring it
awake,

as ecstatic circling birds
could finally croon and tickle
this small wonder
in festive melody,

and long-waiting clouds
shed joys full of eager raindrops
softening atrophied wings,
moistening shriveled legs,

setting this humble dream free
to fly
in wild winds.

TRAILS FOLLOWED

First you make a
trail to follow
away from busy roads,
dropping seeds along the way,

flowers planted
spinning alluring scents
that draw others behind you.

Each flower, each scent
is one you've come to remember
in the arduous dark,

each
you now help others
remember as well.

Follow the trail far enough
and you reach
a still meadow
you can finally rest in,
a place to call home,

living amongst the
butterfly weeds,
lupines,
robins
and dragon flies,

a mosaic of radiant colors,
perfumes and sounds
coalescing in the air.

Slowly you kneel,
hands pressed,
eyes softened,

and breathe,

making yourself known
to the moist ground,

a sacred return
to the land
to live
amongst the living.

ANOTHER DOOR OPENS

Another door opens
inviting me into expanded
horizons,

until I feel confined,
too comfortable,
ready for more.

And another door opens,
a bridge to somewhere
I know not of,
a mystery waiting
to fold me in its arms
even closer,

until again,
restless,
I am ready for more.

And another door opens
I dare go through,
another layer of skin
shed,
left behind,
no longer needed
on this journey,

another tear
fed to the earth,
fresh rawness
revealed,
a place of coming
more fully alive,

until it too
is no longer enough,

not large enough
to house what wants
to emerge,

again,
this unshakable desire for more
pervades me

to melt deeper,
to soar higher,

afraid I am
of this growing longing
and unrest,

of what lies
on the other side,

of what must be left
behind.

And another door opens
into wide open spaces,
my wings stretched
like never before,

my heart breaking
under the most immense
rainfall,

opening childlike eyes
to depth,
beauty,
like no other,

and as day turns to night
and night to day
I reach
even higher
into this
fluid space

until my wings
can take me no further,
pushed I am to the
fine edges
of this great expanse,

again,
feeling empty,
uncertain,
afraid in this place I
no longer belong,

ripe, ready,

the primordial ancestral drum beat
finds me once more.

And another door opens.

WEAVING THREADS

A rare pause
from weary travels
I stop
to face this hole
in the dry desert ground,
the one unwittingly circled
for so long,
deftly,
frantically evaded.

I lower to my
hands and knees
to gaze down,
trembling a bit,
uncertain why,

curiously drawn
into this dark cavernous
space
I cannot see
the bottom of.

Appearing from the
bleak
a single thread
greets me,
swaying gently
in long awaited light,
poking its frail head
cautiously, eagerly,

it rises slowly
from clouded soot
of endless nights past,
the broken promise,
the stained memory,
ascending bravely
for me to behold.

I reach
to meet its wandering head,
gently caressing
its sun-stroked
tender tip
with my own,

when another
unexpected guest
arrives,
peering gingerly
over the edge,
wiggling,
stretching upwards,
offering itself,
longing for my
forgiving touch.

And then more surface,
a family of past trials,
a school of heartbreak,
emerging as one
forgotten rhythm
bestowed in grace,

they rise,
each with their own name
and story,
growing taller now,
dancing lustrously
in fresh wild winds,
an ancient movement
and invitation.

My curious hand
weaves amongst them,

wandering,
winding,
coiling,
twining,
drawn slowly into their
vigorous sway,
into their tales,
these memories
brought to light
from the dark womb
of rich ash below
pulling me in now,
suffusing me
into their dance
of yesterday's sorrow,
fulfilling the promise
of pains past,
enveloping me
into their united cause
to lift and
spiral me upwards
as one banded strand,
within which I am
bound and cradled
above and below,
carried upward
into
a long awaited fabric
of existence
I am ready for.

RETURNING AS

There are paths that haunt me,
calling me through distant
echoes,
from trees and winds
winding me
into unforeseen shadows
of forgotten worlds,

shadows that gradually
bring me into my own,
shadows most others wish to
avoid.

But the heart that perceives
these secret spaces
and hears their nuanced
messages
knows all must soon
succumb,

for it is the nature of things,
the way,

called out as longings of the soul,
long embedded in elder roots,
the core of stones,
and in the deep black
of winter's eyes,

an ageless appeal
permeating all existence,

overwhelming
at times,

as one is taken apart
piece by piece
and made raw again,

a mystery of unfoldment
fed back to the gods.

SWEET BECOMING

In the gradual dispel
of steeped knowing
I find myself losing my
separation with life.

I feel it whispering in my bones,
breathing my lungs,
its swirling winds
dancing in my chest,

its many shapes
twisting and turning
taking flight
through my opening heart.

There is a longing here
to sink further into this
kinship with all things
that sings me awake
from temporary slumbers,
and stirs in wild summer nights
warming me,
ripening me into
fresh new colors of fall
and softening me into
quiet depths of cold winter silence.

There is in me
a growing place where
I no longer exist,
and in that sweet emptiness
I find myself arm-in-arm
as life's own becoming
and beckoning
to all things.

NOBLE CAUSE

At long last
you cry the deepest of pains

washed you are
in tears of generations
who could not give themselves
to their grief

the grief of loss
of abuse
of forlornness
of deceit

the grief of the split between
mankind and
Life

tears held back
wounds untended
for the sake of survival

tremendous grief
now bringing you to your knees
as it must

this your noble cause
your sacred inheritance
taking you alas
to this most noble of moments

to what you have been
waiting for

your crucifixion

your most magnanimous gift to Life

dying to the one Beloved.

THE SWORD

I thought I was the sword
swinging every which way
fiercely driving forward
piercing without shame

scared I was
wounded deep inside
taking up armor
a needed way to hide

until a gentle wind came
ushering me aside
inviting something new
a different way of life

it taught me to soften
to bend like a tree
to let myself fall
what I thought myself to be

slowly I trusted
my hands opened free
the steel slipped downwards
on the floor beside me

a step back or two
from all I had known
this old way of being
of holding my own,

and there I was
a softened man
tears washed clean
undefended again

as when a small child
vulnerable and free
without steeled grip
always protecting me

yet still it was there
this trusted old friend
I couldn't fully turn from
I'd need again

as part of my journey
to use when time
not to grip with dear life
but help me define

you from I
to draw the line
to assert my truth
firm, but kind

faithful when needed
it will always be there
but now there is choice
how, when and where

for now I'm set
in my tender stride
my heart leading forward
my sword at my side.

BELONGING

That last tug
as everything
falls beneath me,

no longer mattering,
no longer mine
to travel with.

It never was.

This dream
has run its course,
its eyes
closed now
as the dark night
turns at its
zenith,

at the point I
no longer belong,
yet belong to
everything.

LEAVING THE TAVERN

There you are
in the dimly lit cavernous tavern
comfortably seated
at a generous round wooden table
surrounded by those you know best,
imbibing the same old clumps of food
and bittersweet brews,
singing your immortal songs
and sharing stories of glory past.

You all partake in the
familial pastime of the ages,
a ritual of belonging
that feeds a part of you
that knows nothing more.

But as the flame flickers
and candle melts
your time-worn traditions
hold less weight in your heart
leaving you progressively
unsatisfied,
unfed,
empty.

Indeed,
your moment has finally come.

A seminal moment of questioning
this veneer existence,
of doubting
the seat upon which you rest so
comfortably.

A moment of
needed uncertainty.

Within the hungry space
of your belly
a soft growl is heard,

the ancient cry,
a portal
to deep longing.

This beckoning encroaches
and presses upon you
without invitation,
slowly filling you,
stirring,

shaking the four pillars
of your sturdy chair,
unraveling the once unbreakable bond
binding you to your brood,
leaving you with heightened restlessness,
a desire,
a thirst
for more.

After much concern
and curious contemplation,
and with a balance of nervous reticence
and excitement,
gingerly
you accept this mysterious plea,
willing yourself to explore and follow the
the larger, winding thread
of this elusive impulse.

And so with strength and courage
you stretch your
stiff waking limbs
and rise,

only to be
abruptly snapped back down
by those seated before you

who question your foolish aspirations,
condemn your impetuous selfishness,
and declare to unmistakably know
what's best.

Your will is tested.

Despite valiant efforts
to conform and comply,
the feeling,
the bursts of longing,
have now captured your will,
and again
you stand,
you stand for the ages,

defying
the piercing glares,
the desperate cries,
the howls of guilt and shame,
the banging fists,
the tight tangled clench
of your wrist.

You stand,
heart pounding,
fiercely resolute.

And with fear's steel grip
fastened in your chest,

and the heavy noise of remorse and dishonor
echoing through the well-tread
corridors of your mind,
you turn
and walk away.

Free at last,
scared,
you wander fresh, attentive,
through the empty spaces
between all things,

determined to offer room
for the
invisible guiding rhythms
to burgeon
and beat louder in your chest.

Here,
chair nor table anchors you,
nor do drinks, stories and songs
dull your widening senses
keeping ancient longings
at bay.

Yet, it isn't long
before the swindling surreptitious voice of
reason
becomes unbearable.

Like those at your table,
it knows best
and directs you away from
meandering unknown spaces
calling you

and towards what it perceives as
refuge,
secure settlement at another table.

A new home.

But with time, courage
and sharpened clarity
you learn to see these
thoughtful intruders for what they are
and drop the sword of discerning felt-sense
through their deceptive screen
availing yourself back
to the space between.

Yet time and again,
even harsher winds of
trickster thought gust through the
vulnerable blackened tavern of your mind,
scorning your decision to leave your table,
inciting you to immediately return,

conjuring idyllic images of being
welcomed back
into the waiting arms of those
who love you,
and of placing yourself on your
firm reliable cozy chair,
clearly,
where you belong.

Swept away
by haunting torrents of
compelling narratives,
by and by

you slowly learn to re-orient yourself
back to calm center
where you grant greater faith
to the stirrings of the quiet one within
than to gorging deceptive fears.

A rebellious pilgrimage indeed,
you are led along winding paths
by irrational optimism,
by unknown knowing,

by something mysterious
wanting you.

As time passes
and with each blind step
a warm presence flowers
in your chest,
its light
teasing the corners
of your eyes.

Something is taking hold of you,
pervading your very being,
bending perception
with light and dark,

twisting and breaking
the stories
you walk by.

Nothing has changed
yet everything has changed.

You wander by unfamiliar
tables,

yet smell the same old brews,
hear the same banal narratives,
and see the same tiring charades

more clearly now,
with ever-widening senses,
their vacantness,
what they are not,

perceiving tiny, shallow, desperate worlds
tightly wrapped in them.

And so you carry onwards
not knowing what else to do,
clear on what you move
against,
uncertain of what you move
with.

As you release yourself further
from the predictable charm of
table and chair,
song and story,
and as warmth nestles more deeply
in your burnishing chest,
so too does darkness
enfold itself upon you
even more,

the dim shallowness of the tavern
finding your own.

Cold
damp
despair

accompanies you
along this bereft pathless path.

Fear and hopelessness
take growing residence
in your vexed mind,
willfully calling out the absurdities
of your direction,
calling more loudly
for you to return
at once.

You are torn, plagued,
as the bleak unknown
swallows you
relentlessly.

Again, though,
somehow
you find it within you
to continue,

the unexplainable
usurps the explained,
growing irrational feeling
outweighs the antiquity of
reason's ways.

Like a rising beam of clarity
intensifying through
the thickening
of fog's convenience

you know

that in no way
could your
old wooden table
ever be enough.

You would not be happy there.

It,
like all the tables you've skirted,
is no longer large enough
to house
the fullness of what you feel
maturing inside.

But now
as dim stale monotony continues,
it seems neither is the
tavern.

Yet, where to turn?

And so you carry on
with
choiceless choice.

Another flicker of the
flame.

Another
footprint.

And just when you think
you cannot walk another inch
along this
droning empty path,

nor hold your
brittling sense of hope
any longer,

you are asked to continue on
even more,
and take yet
one more barren step,

again,
and again,

trudging
without reprieve,
without any sense
of where you are going,
or why,
and when the torment and uncertainty
will end.

This is not what you had
bargained for,
your battered mind cries,
imploring.

It is not what you imagined it
to be.

You would not have left your
secure table
had you known you'd be circling
nowhere
for so long.

But you did leave.

You were unwittingly conscripted
and now you are in a dogged fight
for something
you didn't sign up for
and that you carry within,

breath by breath,
blow by blow,

an ageless battle
between your inner table
and the widening lanes,

between your sturdy chair
and the unsteady way,

a battle that only
thickens and boils
with each step,

a battle the hard-wielding
serpents of thought
are losing.

You are now past the point
of no return.

The biting seductiveness
of your mind
is tenacious,
but the forces of your
uncompromising center
are stronger,
far wiser,

stubbornly refusing to submit
to the old stories,
to dismay,
to your back-breaking
humanity,

refusing
to allow you to turn back,

only to stoke the fires of
anger,
swell the waters of
grief and resentment,
crystalize ideas of
victimhood and powerlessness
even more.

You are trapped,
held captive by something
you cannot see,
you cannot understand,
you cannot deny,
nor escape from,
and that's leading you
to your destruction.

Who are you?
you now wonder.

*What is the **you**
you are fighting for?*

You stumble,
wretched.

Your feet,
your will,
worn.

The unbroken space
unbearable.

The fierce charring crucible
has done its work.

In utter despair
you finally sink to your knees
on the scarred wooden floor,
yielding,
folding,
falling,

knowing
there is nothing left to do
and nowhere else to go.

You are overcome,
buried
in thick shadows of grief and doubt.

And with a long
heartbreaking exhale
the bottomless void of darkness
consumes you in full.

It is then that a
strange flicker of distant light
captures your attention,
one encased
by an ominous vast gloom.

Slowly,
cautiously,
curiously,
you peer ahead.

Move!

Your heart leaps
compelling you forward,
sensing,
suddenly,
your time is near.

With each exhausted step
the screaming winds bare their pointed teeth
with sheer fierceness
gnawing you,
frantically trying lure you back
to where you belong,
askewing your attention
with every wily ruse in their arsenal.

Questions relentlessly echo
through the
tattered corridors of your mind
louder,
the same questions,
the same desperate cries those you loved
hurled at you upon your departure
long ago,
the same ones
bandied through your mind
countless times.

The old food and drinks
deliciously
dance across your taste buds,
tempting.

The familiar
sweet songs and stories
ring heavenly
through your ears.

Just as the clatter of thought
becomes insufferable,
a roaring flame ignites,

uncontrollable fire
spreads across your chest
burning away what last
remnants of hope and reason
you have.

Your pulse quickens,
your heart consumed,

ablaze,
unbearably,
throbbing,
breaking
open.

The gate stands before you now,
beckoning.

It *dares* you to enter
in full.

Your body shudders,
a last gasp of fear,
an urge to look over your shoulder
one last time.

The table,
the tavern,
could never have rested tightly
against the throb of your
chest.

They were never
yours
in the first place.

All those who sit within
this cavernous womb of existence
are part of a
sensuous spell
of storied unfolding,

and yet
all transcend it
and behold it
from worlds unknown.

You are the long breath of life
hinting
of another time,

whispering
discreet words
in the wildness of
empty spaces.

You are the heated interplay
of life's longing
to hold
its warm body in full
once again,

a tapestry of existence
woven within the fabric of the
mighty thick walls
of the tavern,
and beyond.

Yet,
your time has come.

The spell must be
broken.

There is
no turning back.

The ancients
call you home.

Gratitude

I give my gratitude to the wise and loving souls who have guided me into the deepest of dark waters and into the light on the other side. The workshop leaders, shamans, healers, therapists, the brave ones following their hearts, making it easier for others to do the same.

Thank you to my dear friends—the ecstatic dancers, the hikers, the improvisers, the tea drinkers, the seekers—for the small and large ways you have contributed to my unfolding. Each of you has helped me open my heart and make wild empty space for these poems to arise.

Anna Wolff, you have so keenly, confidently and professionally taken charge of the interior and cover with your usual creative magic. Thank you!

To those I've had the honor of presenting to in my keynotes, playshops and webinars, and those in my private practice, my dreams are alive because of you.

Heart-felt gratitude to my beloved Erica. Among many other things, you have taught me to more deeply feel, respect nuance and appreciate beauty. Thank you for helping me mature my soul and refine its expression into poetry.

Finally, to my parents and sister. Through tears of sorrow and joy, slowly, we've learned to find one another. Thank you for seeing me, for loving me, for your dedication in bridging me to what I came here to do.

About the Author

Vince Gowmon has made an arduous pilgrimage to be where he is today. Significant childhood adversity, followed by years of isolation, acute financial hardship, and chronic, undiagnosable pain have all shaped him and his fierce, timely message. Again and again he has entered the deep, dark well of his grief and trauma, forgone conventional living to risk stepping into the unknown, and boldly risen with an opening heart, welcoming the stirrings of Mystery, of what Life wants for him. His talks, writing, music and more are a testament to what he has endured and learned, to who he has become along his winding adventures.

Vince is a popular presenter of keynotes, playshops and webinars. He travels extensively leading on topics such as Leadership, Creativity, Intuition and Play, and is regularly praised for the fun, interactive and experiential nature of his events.

Vince trained as a Certified Professional Life Coach through one of the world's top accredited somatic-based coaching programs, The Coaches Training Institute, and their Co-active Space Leadership Program. He also received advanced training in Organization and Relationship Systems Coaching through the Centre for Right Relationship. In a past life Vince earned a Bachelor of Business Administration from Simon Fraser University. Currently he is studying somatic therapy.

When Vince is not wearing his professional hat or writing in front of his computer you may find him in the ocean, on a mountain, leaning against a cedar tree, letting loose on the dance floor, or making music with his beloved guitar.

For complete information on Vince, visit www.VinceGowmon.com.

You can also find him on Facebook, Twitter, Linkedin and via his Youtube channel.

Made in the USA
San Bernardino, CA
06 March 2018